# MOONLESS GRIEF

# MOONLESS GRIEF

# SALLY ALBISO

MoonPathPress

Poetry
ISBN 978-1-936657-36-0


Cover photo: by John Albiso

Author photo: by John Albiso

Design: Tonya Namura using Catalina Clemente (display) and Gentium Basic (text)

MoonPath Press is dedicated to publishing the finest poets of the U.S. Pacific Northwest.

MoonPath Press
PO Box 445
Tillamook, OR 97141

MoonPathPress@gmail.com

http://MoonPathPress.com

*For John, who first read these poems*

## Acknowledgments

The following poems first appeared in the publications listed below:

"Water Witching" on The Olympia Poetry Network

"In the Mouth of the Released" and "Wildfire" in *Common Ground Review*

"Atonement," "Compass," "Elegy," "Flocking Birds," "Housing the Sacred," "Pacing the Edge of Wilderness," "Red Birdhouse," "Seabird," "Stigmata," "The Notion of Wings," "Tutelage," "When You Visit," and "Where Gulls Keen" in the chapbook *The Notion of Wings* (Finishing Line Press, 2015)

# Table of Contents

## III. IN A PARALLEL LANE

# MOONLESS GRIEF

# I.
# PACING THE EDGE OF WILDERNESS

## When You Visit

firs dim against a drifting sky, crows beat west
eclipsing the horizon. A hush sifts
down the hall. Night fills the breaches
between trees, a lunar crescent ascending

like an illustration in the stories you read me,
earth listing. The next morning
fog lifts like a memory slowly unveiling.
Blue herons stalk the shore stabbing at water

as if it were flesh through which flesh is pulled
delivered into light from a fluid darkness.
Kingfishers kite with a nervous energy like yours.
I ask if you remember dancing

with abandon spinning me into shadow
then sun, our faces transparent as the eggs
I incubated for school waiting for cracks
to appear. Each stumbling chick

we placed into a cushioned box later found
dead, necks broken when they tried to escape
their cardboard nest. How we knew even then
we couldn't save each other.

## Water Witching

The forked stick in his hands
lures him toward the broken pipe's seeping
like a shark dowsing prey
from under sand, the movement
toward subliminal weeping,
what weeks of digging might never have found.

And if I'd sought your ovaries
with a divining rod, my arms tugged
toward their polluted draining,
you might still live, mostly water after all.
What we float in before birth,
lit and throbbing like navigational markers.

The dowser advances
holding the splayed limb before him
as if blinded, feels for the earth's magnetic pulse,
a tide rising beneath his fingertips.
And whether divination or what the body wills,
the wand points down.

But your dying coursed on,
undetected. Your malignant wellspring
crushed organs like pipes
beneath layers of rock, belly
gravid with weight. Your bruised tubing
removed long ago, the ovum from which I sprung

twisting like that branch in the dowser's grasp.
A reckoning I can't ignore,
able at last to stop the flooding
now I've found its source:
all that lies beneath the surface
sustaining, destroying.

## Sanctuary

When Gabriel appeared,
a fanning of wings, a radiance

Mary didn't recognize—the angel's voice
neither human nor bird, his shadow—

did she know then that favor has its price?

Her womb filling with fear
cold as the marble where she's carved

large and Jesus small
as if still a boy, limbs prone

across her lap, wounds

barely visible. How your tumor returns.
But not before we see Moses with horns,

his right arm draped over the tablets,
left arm tensed with raised veins

as if he's just descended Mount Sinai

in sight of the Golden Calf.
We revisit St. Peter's, the Pietà.

*No sanctuary but in sorrow,* you say
gazing at the statue named Pity.

But for whom—the son? the mother?

## The Pretty One

my aunt, prized
for her physical perfection,
long white hands like a pianist.

Were great things expected of her?
She eloped, love-lost,
chain-smoked, laugh turned to cough.

You equated beauty and men
with sorrow. I plant lilacs,
scatter ash to sweeten the soil,

move them into full sun.
They've yet to bloom,
the heady scent you recalled:

your sister blowing smoke rings,
fine lines spoiling her mouth,
fingers and teeth yellowing

like the curtains, bed smelling
of ash. You warned about passion,
sniffed at my clothes,

searched my room, confronted
me with matches as proof of fire.
But I didn't have the looks

to burn, still wait for budding
lilacs, their fragrance
I'll place at her grave and yours:

who loved too much,
mourned spring.
That fervent flowering. Its ruin.

## Compass

A thrush hits the window,
seamless expanse confused for sky,

lies on the ground stunned and panting,
roosts among the branches of my fingers,

my face a fleshy firmament above—
slowly awakens as if freed from a spell.

Yet just as it's released,
another thrush strikes the same glass.

I cradle the bird the way some people pray
but take only silence into my hands,

conceal its body in the woods.
I drive to see you one last time—

your hospital room papered like dusk
in pink and mauve, a view of roses beyond,

their buds, their thorns. You never wake,
shuttered lids tinged green as the sky

when I leave, look north across water
while ships move east into harbors

or west toward the great circle route,
mountains to the south making everything small.

# Seabird

All night ships beat through fog
and plow on calling to each other,
plaintive as gulls. All night, mother,
you perch at the foot of my dreams,

assume a cormorant's dark profile,
wings raised as if they're wet,
a fishy scent lifting when you groom
your breast. In the Everglades I saw

Anhingas—cormorant-like,
some call them snakebirds—
long necks plying water's surface
waiting to strike. You might have

become part snake yet able to fly
from your body's betrayal,
malignancy hissing through cells,
*Eat this.* You stretch your neck,

gaze at me as if I were shadow
moving under water, the dark
tasting of sea, all that returns
unbidden. Cormorants use

parts of dead birds in their nests.
What would you gather
from my prone silhouette:
strands of hair, sticky bits of flesh,

winging away with me as if I'd never been
born? Come morning the fog lifts.
I descend to the beach
and find a red starfish

exposed at low tide, a fingered heart
I rescue as if yours, carry into deeper water
where cormorants pose
on granite shelves, backs turned to shore.

## Tutelage

Crows flock west,
beat toward the sun's descent
as if roosting below the horizon.
At first light they return east
along roads licking the landscape
like tongues, gather
their scavengers' harvest. One crow

hunches over the birdbath
and christens fledglings
from nests he robs
washing their remains, turns
his glance to me, asks
with the oil-sheen of his crown
whether I'll crumble bread

like bits of flesh,
replace the suet set out for flickers?
Why I prize some birds over him
though he shows me how to forage,
how to fly with viscera in my mouth?
I tutor him on grief,
the anniversary of your death,

sow your grit and ash on wind.
It glances off my face as your voice
once had, that sharp discharge
of anger and laughter
settling like your dust on the tide.
The crow sanctifies his offering in water.
I repeat *bread, flesh, bone.*

## Where Gulls Keen

Nothing more silent than songbirds in winter,
music congealed in their throats
only a leafing green will free

and they months away from release
as if such stillness were real

and awakening a dream.
I once lived in perpetual summer, my eyes
accustomed to light, a constancy

others envied while I craved wool
furred against my skin,

nails hidden beneath gloves. I left
blistering cliffs behind, their mesquite burn
seeping west toward the Pacific

where gulls keen and you
raised your palm in a tentative goodbye,

grew small. I faced north
where mountains flare into flower
and the seabirds' requiem is still heard

above frozen hillsides. A clear radiance
emerges like a backlit hand.

Time circles wood's heart
and I curl into my own slowed pulse
like a heron hunting in the shallows,

fish below the surface
rooted to their dark inertia. I wait

for chorusing birds
to herald sun's yield, the furrowed glare
of water to draw me

toward its edge, reach the shore
again and again.

## Ursus Americanus

Close to the road a sow and cub
dark as shadows in the fullness of sun
ignore me, my hulk of car,

edge closer never looking up
though my smell escapes
through open windows. The bears graze
engrossed with their lush temptation.

Other vehicles hurtle past
and still they forage, knee-deep in sedge,
abate their lengthy abstinence.

Then a lone cyclist
and the sow lifts her head, mouth dripping
with lilies, moves into the underbrush
cub at her heels. What spooked her?

That human silhouette
distinct from any car, yellow
jersey blazing like the tag in her ear?

A leafing void begins
where those dusky backs bent.
I lean toward their absence
as if to follow, go down on all fours,

belly ripening like alpine meadows,
and learn to sleep through winter,
give birth, the sun suckling

at the entrance to my den.
How I'd rise ravenous with dreams,
lead my young into light
knowing what to eat, who to fear.

## Pacing the Edge of Wilderness

The prison guard takes a seat in back,
another uniformed presence, bookends

the driver as if we passengers are his charges, our gaze
a felony he can't meet, unused to eye contact—

the implied threat mirrored there—
doors shutting behind him, accurate as guillotines.

What's severed from a man whose days become
a standoff between good and evil

and sometimes those roles reversed, his hands fisted
even in sleep? The guard stares straight ahead.

Watchtowers of cedars flash by, mountains and ocean
thwarting escape from the prison they border.

Safer to remain inside where predators are seen, nights
lit like day, the stalking silence

beyond those locked doors. A young mother
and her baby face the tunneling rush of road

furred with moss from incessant rain
as if all weeping gathers here. The baby cries.

She offers her breast as the bus rocks on,
asphalt unspools like a thread she's pulled

leading to the caged. Is it her child's father
she'll visit? His eyes like flushed birds

glancing off the partition
between them. The baby girl she'll hold up

as he looks down. We watch the bus pull away
toward the prison, stay behind on this beach,

neither guards nor inmates
though you're a mother and I a daughter.

Gulls mass downwind. Something has died—
a seal, plucked sockets facing the tide.

We linger over its mounded bulk
as if mourning a carcass

of our dead, sway like scavengers
above rotting remains, pace the edge

of wilderness. Trees uprooted and tossed about
like nothing the earth can hold.

## Cantor

Long ago, wolves sang here
with such triumph they were destroyed.
Now coyotes penetrate the dark
with their hunger, reach through glass,
and this hour's supplication still greater,
its tenor both animal and human.
Is it the Sasquatch of local lore
bellowing as if to make ears bleed?
Roosting among cedars like a bird
crying out for another of its kind,
bipedal stance encouraging a tongue
that ladles words?
Or can it only hoot and scream,
be taught to sign with furred hands
that shatter a two-way mirror?
The howling continues to gnaw at wind.
I lean toward the voice,
let it wash over me like a moonless grief,
listen as if I might answer.

## Atonement

Some don't clean their teeth on Yom Kippur,
lest they swallow water, their fast broken,

breath ripe as a year's worth of sins.
I brush as if guilt might camouflage

beneath mint, though that pardon soon spent,
my right hand a litany of failings.

How I loved too little or too much,
turned away from the tenacious hold

of want, or even beauty—
the song a beggar proffered in the shade

of a cathedral where no flocks intoned
among denuded hillsides,

just a boy, his head thrown back,
throat exposed to anyone who'd listen,

palms cupped and reaching. I recite
my transgressions, consider birds.

How they beat above me so close
I feel their push and pull,

might pluck their hymns from air,
the mouth of a boy, let song spill

like seed from the throat of my hands. Sin
such a human notion and forgiveness—

Chagall painting *The Sacrifice of Isaac*
as absolution. The son naked

against a bed of logs, his father awash
in red streaming from a corner

of the canvas where Jesus carries his cross,
shadowed figures wait

for the angel's intervention. That messenger
tinged blue as mouths congealed by prayer.

No need for sons bound to wood,
their blood descending

but for mercy's stain—the angel, the ram
partially hidden behind a tree.

## Crossing

Water before me like a trial,
I drive onto the floating bridge
joining one peninsula to another,
glassy passage to my left,

chop to my right as if there's a choice
between smooth current or rough
when so much depends on wind.

I study the lowered sky
balanced above mountains, am reminded
of Dante. How I might profit
from his purgatory:

a giant stone on my back to stoop
beneath pride; eyes sewn shut
to avoid envy, learn patience.

The bridge opens to allow a tug transit.
Gulls call like flocks of pallid prophets
hanging from their cross of sky.
I turn off the car, step out

like the other drivers, a procession
of pilgrims leaning over water
as if divining the future

reflected there. The tug tows its barge
like a punishment, slowly reaches the bridge
as if struggling toward pardon. How long
will we remain in limbo

before we're released from the midpoint
where the unbaptized wait, needing to be held
by something other than that grey light?

# Foxes

Some the color of oxidized metal,
others charcoal as night's descent,
dun as the headlands
or stippled like calico cats
begging with domesticated eyes
for me to pull a rabbit from my hat.

I think of the human inbred,
how the best, the worst traits rise
when bloodlines remain too close—
one Kentucky family tinged blue
as if oxygen-deprived, an attribute
among cousins who married,

an indigo stain in a blushing world.
The perceived superiority
of royal cousins also leading
to blue-blooded consequence,
some dynasties hemorrhaging
as others drooled—

and the foxes grew docile,
instinctual trepidation mottled
as their fur; a cobalt dye
turned the Kentucky kin pink,
while I only dream of a life
with no fear, no shame.

# Sounding

The blind man makes his way,
dark glasses shielding him
from other eyes, white cane tapping
side-to-side as if testing the air's liquidity.

He palms his guide dog like light.
I weigh darkness, a mind devoid of image.
How colors might be tasted or felt:
greens and blues cool as gelatin

quivering in the mouth,
yellows and reds flaring like temper,
black a hand pinning eyelids,
white, their release.

Born small, I could have been blinded
and placed in an incubator
with too much oxygen, grown deaf.
I hold my breath, cover my ears

but the thrum of blood beats
against my palms, the sibilance
and labials of my name forced
from my throat as if spoken

under water. The blind man paces
deliberately. I close my eyes,
light seeping beneath,
the burden of hearing and sight.

# Seraphim

Wings folded against their backs
the weight of sanctity, bodies

real and insubstantial as snow,
voices like the highest notes played

on a violin, such music.
Those we know by name—

Michael escorting Adam and Eve
out of Eden, foretelling the future

of their sons; Gabriel announcing
every birth, the cleft in a human lip

from his touch. How we enter the world
crying from that caress, its remove;

Raphael appearing as a shepherd
guiding us to the underworld.

Hades the same limbo, heaven, hell.
Its ancient rivers of oblivion.

Even among the celestial, a hierarchy—
those who sing praises and burn,

who keep order, provide miracles,
listen to our petitions

for rain, sun, a moment's grace.
Their heads cocked

with canine devotion, eyes
never leaving us, their pity.

# II.
# HOUSING THE
# SACRED

## An Immediate and Reciprocal Pronouncement

*Love you,* I say readily these days,
in person, on the phone, in messages,
my exposed heart pulsing.
When did I begin trading in affection,
a current artifice, universal need?
I used to utter *Take care,*
acknowledged the frailty in any encounter,
penned *Yours Truly* like a vow
while mere convention.
Is this what love has become?
An immediate and reciprocal pronouncement
like exchanging names?
My family didn't voice their fondness,
ended calls and gatherings with a caution
or forecast: *Check the oil. Looks like rain.*
Yet I easily declare my attachment
as if I might not have the chance again.
A mantra to ward off an accident,
terrorist attack, lump in the breast.
Still, when I state *Love you,*
it so often sounds like a question.

## Omen

A cardinal wounds the sky's dull flesh,
scarlet letter morning wears
on its breast. Cars climb
this mountain, painted in shades of blood,

the first color recognized by man
stippled on women's lips.
What do the trucks, sedans, bird portend?
Passion? Ruin? Litters carrying brides

to their grooms. Angels of death
winging by door posts.
Beside this track, others signs revealed,
cougar prints trailing like my own.

Should I beg a ride, trust destiny
to cinnabar, maroon,
drivers like prophets on wheels?
Or practice standing still,

becoming larger? I sing,
voice rising like the cardinal's augury.
The cougar waits, might take me
from behind, suffocate as only love can.

## Judas Horse

The mare steps up to the fence,
breath humid as a summer night,

dark eyes consuming light
like dusk, nudges my hands.

Open-palmed, I offer nothing.
She butts the railing, once escaped

through an unlocked gate,
trotted down the street, tail set high,

wheeled round and whinnied
for those left behind—

belly shivering from the release
she won—then feared. Air lush with grass

like the high plains she roamed
until culled. A Judas horse

leading her into a corral,
the herd animal's instinct to follow.

Later I return with carrots,
the mare still waiting at the fence.

How easily we're betrayed
and forgive.

## Prey

A trail through forest, no wind.
Listless cedars border the path.
A squirrel clings to bark

watched by an owl. Crows
wring light from the sky,
begin to mob in frenzied reproach.

The owl remains fixed
as a cedar's dense core.
The squirrel alarms.

No place to hide from a predator
nor among the subterranean
crowds waiting for a train:

a stranger's heart seizing,
knees buckling as if he genuflected
before some cross I couldn't see.

Paramedics jolting his prone body
until it levitated before sinking again
and I walked away

as I do now
never learning if the man lived
or died, the squirrel splayed on a trunk.

## At the Shelter

Dogs, their eyes shadowed
as the drift of a storm,
jump, bark, cower when I approach
bearing the meaty musk of my body.

Some don't raise their heads
but mirror an ancient sorrow
as if I were penned instead. I beg
for them to come close,

sniff at the loneliness they recognize.
A border collie licks my proffered fist
until my hand unfurls.
Have I come for him, he asks,

ready to shepherd me toward safety,
studies my mouth and voice
but not my eyes,
the potential aggression reflected there.

He accepts my alpha status,
would run alongside me if I chose,
night just a loamy field to cross,
the moon lifting like a howl.

He cocks his head as if listening
to the pulse of my thoughts, whines
that he waits, will always love me,
a burden I'm not sure I can accept.

## Every Flame a Moon

Tent caterpillars invade the alders,
bivouac among stripped trunks,
fall to the ground, a sound like rain
muted by bedded leaves.
The trees grow bare as in winter,
their dark centers exposed
like ravaged women, imploring limbs
tethered by massed cocoons
before the caterpillars weave solitary
husks and emerge as moths
to gather in doorways,
batter against windows
I open. Alders become dust
like wings striking glass.
The moths circle a candle
blinded by light leading nowhere.
Every flame a moon
toward which they fly.

## Flocking Birds

Rain turning to sleet, asphalt to black ice.
A grove of alders succumbs to white

like the sky. Contact with the road
slips away. Winter

once just a word to me, snow
only falling in the mountains,

I didn't recognize the concealed
as treacherous,

ice from a stagnant pond
tasting pure as my imagined heaven

though glittering with cloaked disease.
I shrunk to a pinpoint of heat.

My mother wept from shame,
a quarantine notice posted on our door

as if we'd become the poorest of countries
where children routinely died from typhus,

fever's frozen veil I took into my mouth.
The car spins. Crows flock in a murder,

ravens in a conspiracy. What we name
those congregating darkly

as if always on uncertain footing,
snow spiraling like a piteousness of doves.

## Red Birdhouse

The only color on this snow-chastened day.
Sky adrift, bay gone ashy
as a blanched face. No shadows

to distinguish time just a white light lifting
above the feathered impression of a winter wren,
rabbit tracks filling like my own.

I am erased. Footprints no longer
witness to the path I take, water darkening
to pewter, the exact shade I'd use

describing cold to the blind
while they finger the sharp edge of a knife.
I lie down among drifts, wing

arms and legs into a consecrated presence,
let the frozen world take me, so still,
deer might tug at the dark edges of my clothes.

And I dreaming of red bright as blood
on doorposts, the sign
an avenging angel would recognize.

# Housing the Sacred

Dusk and the water molten
as lead passed through fire, sky burning,
crows like black cinders
littering the horizon, their winging

and descent among cedars.
Singly, by twos and threes,
then in a fervent cloud, the crows settle
shadowing further their weighted roosts.

In the morning they crouch
above road kill, tear
at the already maimed, rob nests,
leave behind skeletons

delicate as the finger bones of saints.
Remains I harvest as if a body
can be made whole again, hands
become reliquaries housing the sacred.

The crows move east, west, light's compass
accompanied by gulls pale as bone
among their dim numbers, an eagle
pursued like another sun.

But it's night these acolytes gather—
a shroud, a vial of blood,
martyred rib,
whatever flesh they can worship.

## Stigmata

Late March, tree swallows
grab insects from air,

collect twigs and grasses, build a nest
in the red birdhouse, faithful
as the swallows returning to Capistrano

on Saint Joseph's Day.
The birds circle, relentless as hope.

I pray to the patron of flight
to shield their frantic winging
toward windows.

How their bones could shatter like glass,
bodies grow limp as a host

on the tongue. What to believe?
In the swallows' skill to fly unharmed?
Piety of Saint Joseph,

protector of expectant mothers
and carpenters? The Mission built

by local tribes forced into slave labor,
hands bleeding like the stigmata
of Saint Francis, backs beaten by monks

of his order. The men they called *father,*
who taught them to love suffering.

## Creation

All those eyes. His terrible voice.
He summoned me like a god—
I'd been waiting for a sign—
when the peacock appeared,
tail feathers dragging
like a rendering of sight.
Such prophecy in his deliberate pace
as if he parted water
with every step. The spurs on his feet
could have pierced me
with shame knowledge yields
and his gaze expose my coveting.
But he punished with beauty
lingering long enough
for me to revel in his grace—
then faded away
until I was left with nothing
but the removal of light.

# The Notion of Wings

I'd like to be brave as a fledgling,
trust in the notion of wings,

sing until people stop and listen,
roost like a moon among trees.

But I only serve those who fly,
offer seed, fill the birdbath,

rescue the ones stunned by windows:
a Rufous hummingbird,

neck bent to tail feathers
when it struck at its reflection,

a likeness that couldn't be trusted.
And earlier this week, a hawk,

wing broken by glass,
even the transparent wounding.

I can't save the hummingbird,
flight once frantic as the wringing of hands,

place a leaf over its small body
bright as fresh blood, took the hawk

to have its wing repaired,
returned to the sky to kill again.

## The Arrow That Pierced Me with Unforgiving Love

Clouds take on the color of teeth
stained with wine. A sacrament
I drink even at breakfast
toasting the first admission of sun,

a neural charge to the body
that mimics passion. My smile arcs
into a grimace. My tongue darkens.
Last night the moon bled

and I tenuously sidestepped another
quarrel, mouth opening and closing
like a fist. This morning,
milky shadows croon the hour's lament

and I lower my eyes in avoidance,
taste metal, a cold sear. You study
a diagram of the heart,
its valves that sometimes murmur

with secrets of their own,
its muscle that can stiffen like a jaw.
I suggest substituting a bitten tongue
to pulse behind your breast

or caging a sparrow there,
wings beating against the limits of flesh.
Mother, when you paint your lips red,
I should recognize your smile

as a warning. How the day warms
but makes no pretense of sheltering
and birds become tethered to silence .
I grind between my teeth.

# III.
# IN A PARALLEL LANE

## Storm

and what appears substantial
yielding. The roots of trees
exposed like pulled teeth,
the void a tongue can't shelter.
I could surrender too,
dream through the wet and wind
governed by darkness I don't see.
Crawl into a cave
so time no longer measures
each night. Give birth
while still slumbering
and not feel the swell
of absence. Suckle young,
my milk tasting of the dormant:
bear, marmot, the Common Poorwill.
A hibernating bird,
its flock called an *addiction*
as if flight becomes sleep,
becomes craving
only a season of torpor relieves,
and loss just a word
like winter.

## In the Mouth of the Released

river, hundreds of seagulls bathe,
beat their wings ridding them
of salt, a sound like wind-driven
*milagros* left by the faithful—

tin charms of legs, arms, babies.
What needs mending
or is offered in gratitude
for prayers answered.

The gulls immerse
in communal baptism, so great
their numbers all I see
is frothing white,

the gleam of water buried
like layers of fallen votives.
What is a miracle? A river
undammed? Salmon returning

to pool in the shallows like souls
in limbo, leap upstream
to a martyr's death?
How willingly the fish surrender,

bodies flaring red as coals,
and some pilgrims leave bits
of themselves behind—a hand, foot,
heart beaten out of metal.

## Late June

A mist still veils the sky,
camouflages the horizon in grey
while our daystar hides

and the bay's tin lid won't lift.
Farther south I ignored the sun
annoying in its devotion,

alarming heat that melted tar
and scorched the coastline brown.
But here it rains, even in summer,

morning drab as the doe
grazing on the lawn, indifferent
to the fleshy gathering of clouds.

Better the promise of dandelions
rolled about in the heat of her cud
or the bouquet of daisies

I've picked: a handful
of stars unveiling
their luminous saffron hearts.

* * *

The fuchsias tongues have been torn
from their mouths. The doe lifts
her head, legs unfurling

like the sweetest of buds,
and leaps beyond the retaining wall
leaving her fawn behind to nest

in tall grass. I discover a nest
by the door. All that remains of flight
while trees reach

with the solemnity of mourners
toward that emptiness
other birds shape

and the fawn dozes:
nose a torn map of pink
showing through black, a lump

in its neck that could be an abscess
from some predator's attack.
I would curl beside it,

offer apples as a treat,
but it must struggle alone
against approaching shadows.

Hide where it can and rise scarred
each morning to make a sustenance
of light, however dulled.

## The Vixen

resembles a tattered red dress
stained with drink and smelling

of smoke. Her teats hang perilously
close to the ground. She yawns,

then barks, voice part scream,
part howl. How many nights

has she padded through the dark
alone—the moon a capricious mate

veiled by fog or its own waning
while her pups' appetite

never diminishes? How many nights
have I chased the tail of dreams,

suckled nothing but fear?
The fox pants,

teeth reflecting the early hour
like beached shells.

She paces this shore
to sniff at brine, the taste of salt

in prey's blood. She'll eat
what fate provides

yet trails me like dawn's feral shade
as if I'll rain mice

or the treats meant for dogs.
The vixen approaches,

would crouch above bones,
the crumbs pockets keep,

and barks again,
no whine of supplication—

*Feed me,* she insists,
*though I'll never lick your hand.*

*Then put on your party dress*
*and run red along this beach too,*

*breasts filling with milk,*
*pockets empty.*

# When I Dream of Horses

In fields or corrals,
among the dust motes of stables
and churned mud of racetracks,
wherever I find them,
they draw me close.

Their silhouettes backlit
like the depths of a cathedral.
Their ears and eyes a focused piety.
How they graze my offered palms,
even if empty,

and their alfalfa-scented breath
is a benediction.
The solidity of their flesh is a heat
I can wrap my body around.
When I dream of horses,

they stand among shadows
more shadowed still, sleep
until led by morning's tether
into the fields again—
caught between pastures of sky

and the earth's slow tilt.
In the distance, fences
too high to jump
and a road curving beyond sight
so they close their eyes

to what can't be gained
and drowse with one hoof cocked
or face each other, cheek-to-cheek,
taking comfort among their kind
until forced to bear

a rider's company,
an added burden to carry forward.
When I dream of horses,
I dream of the weight
in people's eyes.

How dilated pupils
become an obscurity that consumes
the way dusk devours the horizon
and faces become fences—
white-washed posts and rails

repeating like the stuttered image
after staring into light.
How I approach those barriers
separating me from the herd
and wait to be recognized.

## Dialogue

You say, *ambulance, Emergency*
*Room, more tests needed.*

I hear quails alarming.

A squirrel also warns
and there'd been other omens.

You brought a spade inside

still covered in dirt.
A sparrow flew into the house

beating against windows

until your pulse splintered.
You say, *arrhythmia.*

I hear flushed quail flee,

a thrumming like a covey of hearts.
Down clings to my shoes,

a trail of fresh blood.

You say, *there's no pain.*
I hear the quail's mate call all day.

## Hunting Rabbits in Snow

When you speak of fall,
you speak of change—
which is really surrender.
Leaves turning to mold
and bulbs burrowing deeper.
Days growing leaden as cedars
bowed beneath freezing rain—
a numbness like hunting rabbits
in snow. How you cried and shivered
and were told to hush,
to suffer the cold. Each kill's blood
an offering, a red flower blooming
against white as crows gathered.
This is how you learned
to feed yourself and not mourn
but didn't teach me.

## For Twenty Seconds

The bed moves with the floor beneath it
as if roused by some impatient hand

though birds still slumber and light
hasn't breached night's gate.

The walls seem to lean in. A cup topples
spilling tea gone viscous as tears

on a cheek. I whisper *earthquake*
as if to speak louder will incite more

tremors. But I control nothing.
A kind of freedom to passively lie here

as windows shiver and books
fall open like palms to be read.

What do they predict?
How uncertain one moment is to the next.

How tectonic plates can bump each other
like people in a crowd

creating shock waves as metal bends,
glass breaks. I could shatter.

Be martyred by arrows of debris
or crushed beneath my hoard

of things, my body fragile
as the shadow it leaves.

No match for falling beams
or even the weight of my own sins.

## Wildfire

The inferno persists.
My skin smolders
and throat flares
with swallowed stars.
Hillsides blaze and birds
are grounded, wings laden

with ash. I dream
of wood, of lightning,
a cigarette's spark.
Coals left undampened
by hunters in a hurry
to remain concealed.

But so little can hide
in a fire. Animals fleeing
into the open
as roofs and walls pant
like living things.
Only chimneys left,

hearths gone cold
and the people
who sat before them,
faces lit. I tongue my lips
but can't stop flame,
grown used to burning.

## Nest

A conical shape concealed
among loops of rope
hanging from a cedar bough.
A shelter of lichen and moss
lined with feathers so soft
I want to peck my way through a shell
and curl inside such refuge.
This way station between hatching
and flight more forgiving
than immediate delivery,
a secondary womb that secludes
until air gives lift. How it would feel
to wake to that mercy and suspend
among cushioned walls
even after the last umbilical scab
falls away. To linger there
until able to take in light
without squinting,
breathe without crying first.

## In a Parallel Lane

someone familiar could be driving
or a stranger I'd like to meet
yet there's too much metal and glass

between us and we might be headed
in opposite directions.

But if I let go of the steering wheel
and wave like a drowning victim,
mouth the word *Stop!*—

if I turn off the engine and get out
of the car to lie down

on the yellow stripe in the asphalt
and position my back
so the broken line goes through it

and I stare at the sky like road kill—
would other vehicles begin to mob

like crows, drivers nudge me
with hands that could be beaks,
their faces emerging

from behind windshields?
Or would the police be called

and I led away and cited
for inertia, for creating
a disturbance? Public loneliness

or impersonation of the dead
not allowed.

## Vocation

How is it we choose our work?
The butcher with his meaty hands

splaying ribs. The cuts he crafts
to create a new order from each body

while growing inured to blood.
The surgeon who carves at flesh

beneath lights so bright
they could be the world's first dawn,

who exposes human hearts
for the muscle they are.

And what of the firefighter
who's intimate with flame.

Is he most alive when fire destroys?
I could become a butcher,

surgeon, firefighter, martyr.
A cloistered mystic

or an itinerant monk, my beggar's bowl
held out to the world.

But I choose to make a profession
of sorrow, a calling of loss,

wear black like a cowl of grief.
In some places white is the color

of mourning so brides dress in red
as if to stain their skin

with whatever joy they can find.
And earlier this week,

even the moon bled
reflecting the sun's last rays,

flared crimson as a wife
burning on her husband's funeral pyre.

## Alone in the House

I watch firs darken into dusk
and birds take to their roosts,
sing themselves to sleep.

Everywhere these drowsing
multitudes while only my shadow

leans into walls,
only my tread answers
down the hall. Is death this dreamless

and solitary? And do we diminish
or enlarge into night? Alone

in the house, I run my fingers
over the surface of wood,
dust insistent as your ash

sown on the tide
and returning again. I gather

a belt, a sweater
to tighten about my waist
like your arm, rest on my shoulders

like your hands.
I look into mirrors as if to catch you

standing behind me.
Your reflected image
like a collection of nesting dolls

that grow smaller and smaller
as they're opened.

# Aves

*Voices Raised As If Prayer*

Geese become shifting geometry
in a plane of sky. An eagle
scans the shore, talons

the size of a man's fists.
Jupiter's Bird, some call it,
the messenger.

What omen does the eagle bring
clutching wind the way I gripped
my father's hand

when we entered the ocean,
our limbs pale as the winging
of gulls, and he lifted me

above the tidal bore
to walk on water, remember
Jesus on his sea alone

cleaving only to a distant father
while mine remained flesh
I could grasp.

*The First Frost*

Jays crowd the feeder.
A maple's exposed limbs bloom
with the flowering

of their wings. The feathered
branches of cedars hang heavily
as a woodpecker traffics

among them seeking others
that bore into wood.
For months, a flicker

has roosted above the bedroom
window. He wakes,
shivers his wings into light.

He drills at rafters
as if to penetrate the pulpy mass
of dreams, the limits of any shelter.

*Another Dawn*

The sun's consolation dim.
Clouds take on the color
of etched granite

like the names I've come to trace,
to replicate on paper
what my mouth no longer can.

In the cemetery, gulls glean
the grass surrounding headstones,
what we bury

leaching back into soil.
A woman at a neighboring grave
bows to me, her shadow

darkening the snow at our feet,
my answering obeisance.
We nod like two cranes

in a courtship dance,
backs to the sky.
We offer the mute solace

of our spines bent in reverence,
the grief bones contain.
The gulls call to each other.

The songbirds keep their silence.
All but the winter wren
that sings no matter the season.

# Elegy

Even small deaths imprint on the eye—
a hawk ambushing a jay,
its blue feathers strewn about
like a sky gone aground, its carcass
I kneel above collecting bones.

Everything grieves—
trees lamenting their loss of leaves
thrashing bare branches against windows
imploring the return of spring, jays
massing nearby screeching

a summons, a communal dirge.
And now a crow,
voice raw as any mourner's,
another crow darkly shadowed
in the street bloodied by cars.

I place the bird in the trash
but its mate protests
as if every sorrow has been unleashed,
must be buried. I dig a grave,
shovel dirt over glazed eyes,

watch from inside
as the keening crow approaches,
paces the turned soil,
bends and lays its head there
listening for the beat of wings.

## About the Author

Sally Albiso earned a BA in Spanish from UCLA and an MA in English with a creative writing emphasis from San Diego State University. While at SDSU, she studied with the poets Glover Davis and Carolyn Forché and completed a thesis of her own poetry.

After receiving her master's degree, she taught English composition, creative writing, and English as a Second Language at Chapman College, San Diego State University Extension, and Southwestern College.

In 2003, Albiso and her husband moved from California to the North Olympic Peninsula of Washington State, where she returned to writing poetry.

She has been nominated for two Pushcart Prizes and received the Jeanne Lohmann Poetry Prize, The Muriel Craft Bailey Memorial Award, the Robert Frost Foundation Poetry Award, and the Camber Press Chapbook Award for her chapbook *Newsworthy*. Two other chapbooks, *The Notion of Wings* and *The Fire Eater and the Bearded Lady,* were published by Finishing Line Press in 2015 and 2016. Her poems have appeared in *Blood Orange Review, Common Ground Review, Crab Creek Review, Floating Bridge Review, Poetica, Pontoon: an anthology of Washington State poets, Rattle, The Comstock Review,* and other publications.

Made in the USA
Middletown, DE
23 September 2020